MORE
NATURE
In Your
BACKYARD

Simple Activities for Children

By Susan S. Lang

WITH THE STAFF OF CAYUGA NATURE CENTER
illustrated by Sharon Lane Holm

The Millbrook Press
Brookfield, Connecticut

Many thanks to Janet Hawkes, Ruth Yarrow, and Linda Speilman of the Cayuga Nature Center, and to Murray McBride, for all their useful comments.

More thanks to my husband, Tom Schneider, and daughter, Julia Schneider, for their love, interest, and support.

Susan Lang

Library of Congress Cataloging-in-Publication Data
Lang, Susan.
More nature in your backyard / by Susan Lang; with the staff of Cayuga Nature Center; illustrated by Sharon Lane Holm.
p. cm.
Includes bibliographical references and index.
Summary: Provides instructions for simple science experiments and nature activities to be performed in the backyard.
ISBN 0-7613-0308-1 (lib. bdg.)
1. Science—Experiments—Juvenile literature. [1. Science—Experiments. 2. Experiments. 3. Nature study.] I. Holm, Sharon Lane, ill. II. Title.
Q164.L254   1998
507.8—dc21   97-32181   CIP   AC

Published by The Millbrook Press, Inc.
2 Old New Milford Road
Brookfield, CT 06804

For Janie Clark—an incredibly gifted and talented fifth-grade teacher at the Caroline Elementary School, Ithaca, New York

Susan S. Lang

For James and Dylan

Sharon Lane Holm

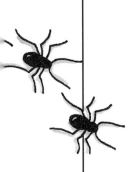

A Note for Preserving Nature

Whenever possible, try to enjoy and not disturb nests, plants, or animals in the woods and fields.

When you do collect any plants, seeds, or flowers, take just a few of a kind, making sure there are plenty left.

If you are catching insects or other creatures, be gentle, and let them loose after you are done with the project.

Do not bother birds that are nesting or feeding, and do not touch or take birds' eggs.

Pick up any garbage you see, and don't leave any yourself!

Contents

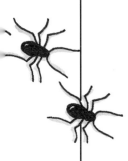

1 Insects and Spiders

The Tree-Shaking Insect Trap

You need:

a big white bedsheet to collect lots of insects, or a shoe or shirt box top lined with white paper

What to do:

Place your box top or sheet under the branches of a bush or tree. Look at the branches—how many insects do you see? Is there a caterpillar on a leaf? A beetle crawling around?

Shake the branches fairly hard, so the insects fall into the box top or onto the sheet.

What happens:

How many insects did you catch? How many different kinds? Did you catch any that you hadn't noticed before? Were they using camouflage to hide? What were they eating?

If you want to observe the insects, use several leaves to pick up the insects and gently put them into glass or plastic jars that have tops with airholes. Give them several leaves from the bushes that they were on and a few drops of water. Don't forget to release them after a few days.

Why:

Because there are insects here, insects there—why, there are insects everywhere! From snowy mountains to steamy jungles, insects have been creeping and crawling all over the world for millions of years. Of all the kinds of animals living on earth, one third are insects! To list all their different names would take 6,000 pages in an encyclopedia. And every year, we find 7,000 to 8,000 new kinds of insects.

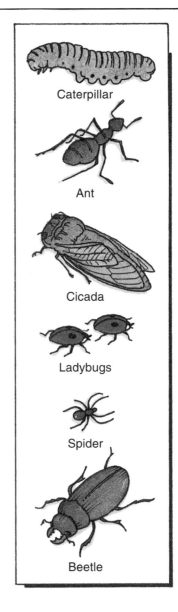

Caterpillar

Ant

Cicada

Ladybugs

Spider

Beetle

The Bug Pit (to catch bugs on the ground)

You need:
4 containers (plastic,
    glass, or cans)
bits of leaves
a digging spoon
several pieces of
    fruit and cereal
4 boards (or tile
    or slate)
masking tape

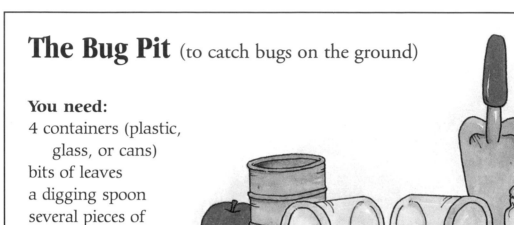

What to do:
Dig a hole large enough to hold two of the containers. (Good places
to try are the lawn, woods, garden, or compost pile.) The top of
each container should be at ground level. Put bits of fruit in one
container and cereal in the other. Add leaf litter to both. Place the
containers in the hole and place two small balls of wadded tape on
the top edge of the containers. Place the boards over the tops of the
containers. (The wadded tape prevents the boards from fitting too
tightly.) Now, bury the other two
containers in an entirely different
place. Fill as before, and cover.
    Check the pits three times
a day.

What happens:

Which container caught the most insects? Why? Examine what you've caught. Any slugs? How many have wings? Are there any beetles (six legs)? Spiders (eight legs)? Ants? Don't forget to remove your pit traps!

Why:

Food attracts insects. Many insects have a very strong sense of smell, usually through their antennae. Some can smell food miles away. To eat, insects bite, lick, or suck to get at what they want. Some will even chew through metal. Although most insects eat plant life, many have adapted to eating other things too, from glue and pepper to fabric, and even other insects.

Who Needs Insects, Anyway?

We do! While it's hard to live with them, we can't live without them! Humans are constantly at war with insects because they attack us, invade our food, devour our crops, and carry deadly diseases.

But we couldn't survive without them. They are food to many animals and even to many people. Insects are also needed to pollinate some crops. Some insects are even used to treat diseases and help scientists make new scientific discoveries.

Insects are also valuable for the honey, wax, shellac, and silk they produce and for helping to clean up dead animals and plants.

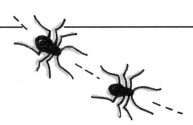

Raising Mealworms

What you need:

several king-size mealworms from a pet
   or bait shop (ask to be sure they haven't
   been sprayed with hormones)
a small jar or clear plastic
   container with holes punched in lid
Mealworm Munchies: Mix together
   6 to 8 cups bran flakes; 1½ cups
   bonemeal; 1 tablespoon brewers yeast;
   1 cup ground puppy kibble; ¼ cup flour, dried bread, or cookies;
   an apple core, sliced potatoes, or oranges
bedding such as dry sawdust, dry leaf litter, or ripped up egg
   cartons
a pencil
a calendar
a magnifying glass
a straw

What to do:

Place some bedding in the bottom of the container and about ½ inch
(1 cm) of mixed up mealworm munchies. Put in the mealworms and
mark the day on a calendar. Keep them warm, dry, and in the dark.
Be sure there's enough food for them to hide under. Observe once or
twice a week for several months to see how they change. Add a
small piece of fruit or potatoes to the jar once a week.

   Once every 3 to 4 months clean the mealworm container by
placing the mealworms in a separate box, washing their container,
and replacing the bedding and food. Don't breathe in the dust!

What happens:

Mealworms are the youngsters or larvae that hatch from the eggs of a grain beetle. Once hatched, they will eat and grow for several weeks to a couple of months. As a larva eats and grows, it gets too big for its own skin, so it will molt—burst out of its skin—sometimes up to 20 times before it begins its pupal "teenager" stage.

In several weeks, while in the pupal stage, the larva will slowly change and grow into an adult beetle. Notice how it eventually changes to brown and then to black. The adult can live for several months. If it's a female, it may lay some 500 eggs before it dies!

The eggs will hatch in one week if you want to start all over again.

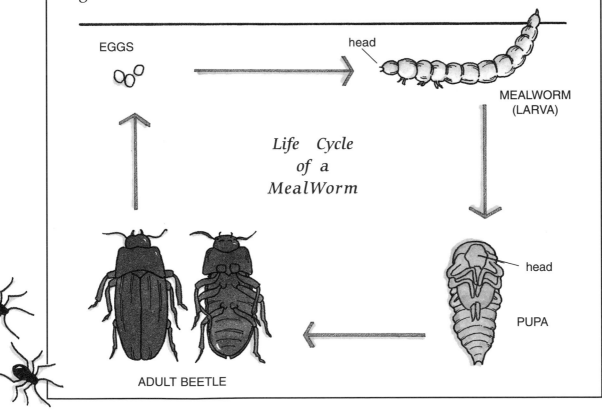

EGGS

head

MEALWORM (LARVA)

Life Cycle of a MealWorm

head

PUPA

ADULT BEETLE

Fun with Mealworms

You need:
5 to 10 king-size mealworms
a shoe box 3 inches (8 cm) high
a magnifying glass
any or all of these:
   cardboard,
   a straw,
   scented
   markers,
   an eyedropper,
   a flashlight, paper

What to do:
Put the mealworms in the box and look at
them closely through the magnifying glass.
How many legs do they have? Do you see any
eyes? Antennae? Hairs? Mouth?

Here are some experiments to try:

Make a wall in the middle of the box with the cardboard. See if
the mealworms go around it.

Using the marker, draw a line in front of the mealworms.

Using the straw, blow on the mealworms.

Drop water around the mealworms with the eyedropper. Put a
drop of water on one.

Shine the flashlight on them.

Fold a piece of paper to make a tent for them.

What happens:

Can you get the mealworms to back up? Do they hide from light? How do they react to touch? What happens when you blow on them? What happens when you draw a line with the marker in front of them? How do they react to water? To walls? To the paper tent?

Why:

Adaptations help living things survive. A giraffe's long neck is an adaptation: It helps the animal reach its food (treetops). How a living thing behaves is also an adaptation. Since many birds eat mealworms, why would moving away from light help the mealworms? If they hide from light, they probably also hide from most birds. Moving away from light is an adaptation.

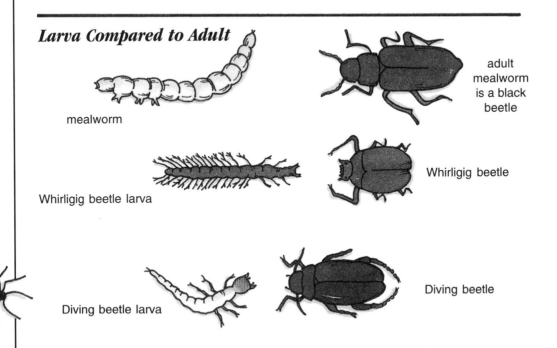

Larva Compared to Adult

mealworm

adult mealworm is a black beetle

Whirligig beetle larva

Whirligig beetle

Diving beetle larva

Diving beetle

Treat a Spider to Dinner

You need:
a flashlight if you hunt at night
a spray bottle of water with
    a fine-mist setting
a magnifying glass
a broom straw or stick
tweezers
pencil and paper
an insect you've collected (see The Tree-Shaking
    Insect Trap and The Bug Pit, p. 6 and p. 8)

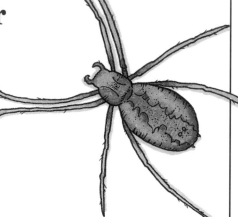

Orb Weaver

What to do:

Go hunting for spiderwebs. In the winter the basement, attic, and garage would be good places to look. If it's fall, spring, or summer, you'll have more choices outside. Look along fences, and in hedges, trees, shrubs, and outdoor light fixtures.

Pick one web to observe carefully with the magnifier. Test it for stickiness by gently touching with the straw or stick. If there is no wind, try spraying a web with a gentle water mist so you can examine it better.

Look for a web that has a spider. Using the tweezers, place an insect gently on the web. Wait quietly to see what the spider does. Return to the web at night with a flashlight—what's happened to the insect? What's the spider doing?

Continue to find as many different kinds of webs as you can and identify them. Can you find funnel webs, sheet webs, triangle webs, globe webs, orb (also known as cartwheel) webs, or just plain irregular (disorganized) cobwebs?

What happens:
You should be able to find several different kinds of webs. Why do you think different spiders make different webs? When you visited the spider again at night, how did it react to the flashlight? What happened to the insect you put in the web?

Why:
Those spiders that weave webs each have a different style, depending on how they catch their prey. In an orb web, a spider waits in the middle with a leg on each strand until it feels movement, and then it runs quickly to bite or wrap the caught insect. Since spiders can only "drink" liquid food, their saliva turns the insect's insides to mush so the spider can suck up the soupy insect guts, throwing away the hard shell, wings, and legs. Although this may sound gruesome, spiders are friends to humans because they eat many insects.

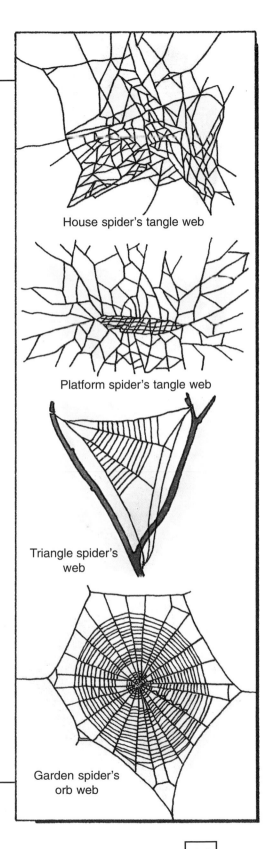

House spider's tangle web

Platform spider's tangle web

Triangle spider's web

Garden spider's orb web

Preserving a Spider Web

You need:

a triangle or orb spiderweb
    (the flatter the spiderweb,
    the better)
hair spray
white or black spray paint
    (if you use white paint,
    use dark cardboard; if you
    use black paint, use white
    cardboard)
    a piece of cardboard
    a pair of scissors

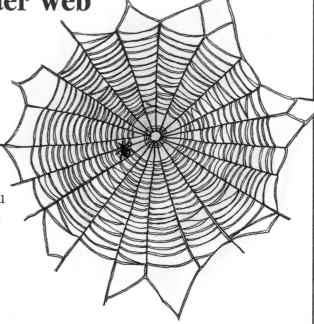

What to do:

Hunt around for abandoned spiderwebs. See Treat a Spider to Dinner (p. 14).

Inside: Check with an adult to make sure you can use the spray paint where you've found a web, and take whatever precautions you need to. Holding the hair spray about 1 foot (0.3 meter) from the web, spray the web lightly. Let dry and repeat with spray paint. Slide the cardboard behind the web. The paint has made the web sticky. Slowly and gently press the cardboard to the web until you have a nice impression on your board. With the scissors, snip the anchoring strands of web.

Outside: Look for a big, flat web and spray it very gently first with the hair spray, then with the paint. Place the cardboard behind the web and snip the anchoring strands of web.

If you like, when the paint has dried you can cover your project with plastic wrap.

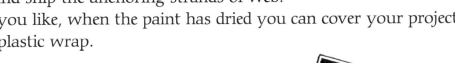

cardboard

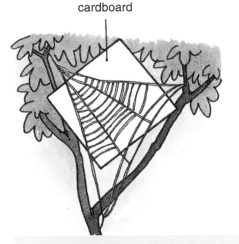

Spiders and Silk

Spiders come in many shapes and sizes, but they all have eight legs, two body parts, and fangs to capture and often poison their prey. And they all spin silk. Using liquid silk from thousands of tiny "faucets" in their abdomen, spiders handle the silk with their little claws, producing both sticky and nonsticky strands. The liquid silk dries as soon as it hits the air. Most spiders can make different kinds of silk, for traps, to weave into a web, to protect eggs, to tie up prey, to walk on, and, for some spiders, to hang from so they can be carried by the wind.

2 Birds

Food Fit for the Birds

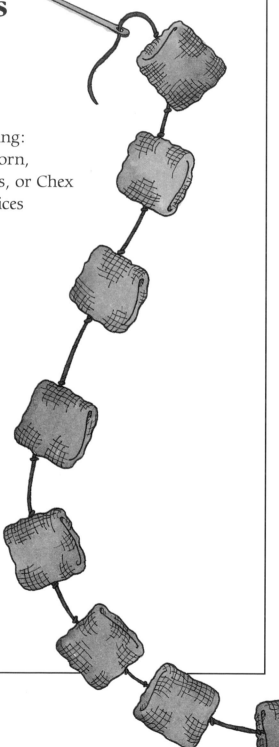

You need:

a strong needle
heavy thread, cut in three 1-yard
    (1-meter) lengths
one cup each of three of the following:
    unshelled peanuts, popped popcorn,
    raisins, cereal (such as corn pops, or Chex
    squares), stale bread, or apple slices

What to do:

Thread the needle and using only
one type of food per thread, evenly
 space the food by knotting each
 piece in place, leaving 1 inch
 (2.5 cm) between each morsel.
 Hang each line from a tree close
 to a window.

What happens:

Chances are the foods will
attract birds. What kinds of
birds come? Which foods are the
most popular? Do some birds go
for one food and other birds for
another? Which food disappears
the quickest?

Why:
Different birds like different foods. Woodpeckers and nuthatches like fats (such as meat drippings that harden, peanuts, and peanut butter). Sparrows, juncos, cardinals, and finches prefer seeds. Robins, mockingbirds, and cedar waxwings like fruits. Chickadees and titmice like a variety of foods, and hummingbirds like sugar water or water and honey. Many birds will also dine on leftovers, such as bread, crackers, doughnuts, cookies, dry dog food, cooked pasta, some vegetable scraps, and even mealworms.

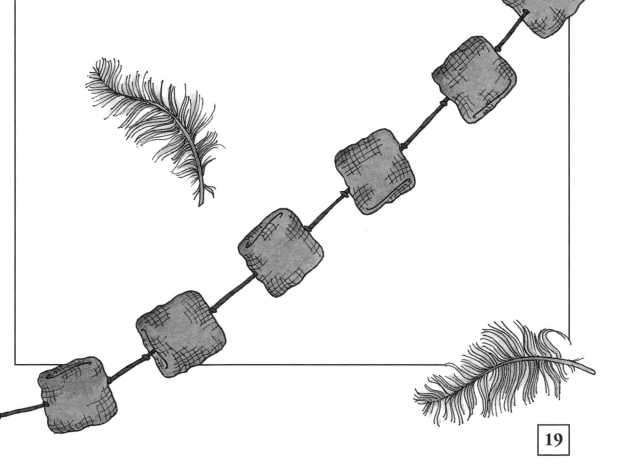

Feather Zip and Lift

You need:
a flight feather
a magnifying glass
a pin
a pencil with an eraser
a hair dryer

What to do:
Examine the feather with
the magnifying glass. Is it a
feather made for flying or just for
keeping the bird warm? Many birds have two kinds of
feathers—the firm, flexible flight feathers that are waterproof
and lay in tight layers over the bird, and the soft and fluffy ones
that are near the body. Why do you think they're different?

Assuming you have a flight feather, notice how its "barbs" seem
"zipped" together. Pull a few apart and see how they act as little
hooks. Now stroke them back together. Can you make the feather
look smooth again?

Place the feather on a table. Does the feather curve? Hold the
feather so it curves down toward the table, and stick the pin in
where the feathers begin on the quill. Then stick the pin in the pencil
eraser. Make sure the feather can move loosely on the pin. Turn the
hair dryer on high (check with an adult to make sure you can do
this) and blow the air over the top of the feather. Does it move?

Take the pin out, turn the feather upside down, and repeat the
hair dryer step. Does the feather move now?
Which way: up or down?

down
feather

flight
feather

What happens:

Chances are, the feather lifted up in the first experiment but not when it was upside down in the second experiment.

Why:

The reason the feather lifted is the same reason why airplanes fly: because the feather (or airplane wing) is curved, air travels over the curved top faster than it does underneath. That difference in air speed creates upward lift.

The soft furry feathers of a bird are the down feathers (have you ever heard of a down quilt?). These cozy fluffy feathers are like long underwear, keeping the bird warm but not useful for flying.

As feathers wear out, they fall off and birds grow new sets of feathers. This happens at least once a year.

quill

barbules

3 Snow, Sun, and Ice

Pure White Snow . . . or Is It?

You need:
snow on the ground
3 paper towels
3 plates or pieces of cardboard
3 cups
a magnifying glass

What to do:
Place a paper towel on each
plate. Choose three different
locations from which to take
a sample of snow, such as
the side of a road (ask an adult to go with you), under trees, a
windowsill, or tree limb. Put a cup of snow from each location on
the paper towels. Predict which will be the dirtiest and which the
cleanest.

When the snow melts, examine the paper towel with a
magnifying glass.

What happens:
You probably found many particles in the snow, even though it looked clean.

Why:
Although snow looks pure white, it's loaded with dust, salt from the oceans, and soil particles. Air and clouds are also loaded with these particles. In fact, these little impurities—some require a microscope to see—are the kernels of many snowflakes. As air gets colder, wet air forms clouds of droplets that may freeze more easily onto a particle. As soon as this ice crystal hits a supercool water droplet, a snowflake is born.

Sweet Snowy Treats

You need:

the ingredients for the recipe you choose

a fresh snowfall: If you live in a city,
　　try the Pure White Snow
　　experiment (p. 22) to see if the
　　snow is clean enough to eat

2 bowls (1 to collect snow, 1 to mix recipe)

a mixing spoon

Snowy Ice Milk

1 cup milk

1 "egg" (Use a liquid egg product, not real eggs.
　　Follow the directions to measure one egg.)

½ cup sugar

dash of salt

1 teaspoon vanilla

Blend the above well and add clean, fresh snow until
it's absorbed. Enjoy!

Snowy Ice Cream

1 cup cream

½ cup sugar

1 teaspoon vanilla

dash of salt

Blend and mix in some clean snow.

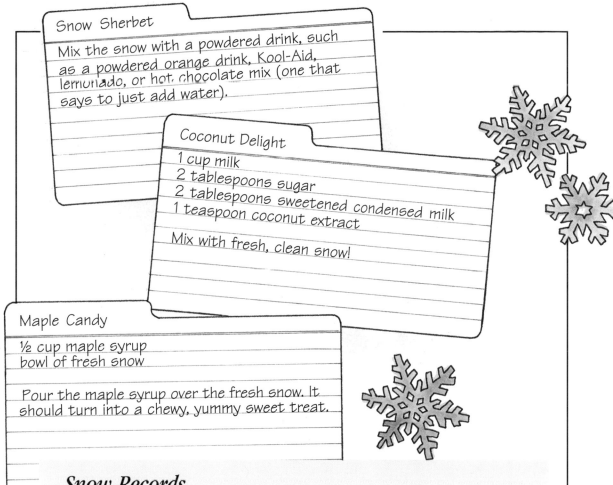

Snow Sherbet

Mix the snow with a powdered drink, such as a powdered orange drink, Kool-Aid, lemonade, or hot chocolate mix (one that says to just add water).

Coconut Delight

1 cup milk
2 tablespoons sugar
2 tablespoons sweetened condensed milk
1 teaspoon coconut extract

Mix with fresh, clean snow!

Maple Candy

½ cup maple syrup
bowl of fresh snow

Pour the maple syrup over the fresh snow. It should turn into a chewy, yummy sweet treat.

Snow Records

What's the most snow that's fallen in one season in the United States? The record is 1,122 inches (2,850 cm) from 1971–72 on Mt. Rainier in Washington! That's more than 93 feet (28 meters). Imagine fifteen tall men standing on top of each other!

What's the record for the amount of snow that's fallen in one day (24 hours)? 76 inches (193 cm) in 1921, in Silver Lake, Colorado. That's 6 feet, 3 inches (190 cm), which is the height of one tall man.

If White Is the Coolest Color, What Is the Warmest?

You need:
3 pieces of colored paper,
    1 piece of black paper,
    all the same size
    a sunny winter day
        with snow on the
        ground but without
    a lot of wind
8 forks or spoons
a kitchen timer

What to do:
Place the four sheets of paper on the snow in the sunshine.
Weigh the paper down with the spoons or forks. Check in ten
minutes. Has the snow begun to melt under any of the papers?
Check again in twenty minutes.

What happens:
One of the papers will probably melt into the snow much
sooner than the others. Which color do you think it will be?
What color clothing keeps you the warmest in the winter?
What colors keep you the coolest in the summer?

Why:

Black absorbs sunlight, while white reflects it. The black paper absorbs the sun's warmth, which melts the snow. The snow under the white paper probably stayed the same.

Black and White

A polar bear has white fur for camouflage, but its skin is black. Can you guess why?

Making a Snow Catcher

You need:

a piece of black fabric
    (black velvet is ideal)
a piece of cardboard
glue or tape
a popsicle stick or other kind
    of handle (a stick, a dinner knife,
        a wooden spoon)
        a magnifying glass (chilled in
        the refrigerator so it doesn't fog
        up outdoors)

What to do:

Make the snow catcher ahead of time:
Glue or tape the fabric onto a piece of cardboard.
Glue or tape the cardboard onto a handle. Put
the snow catcher in the freezer and wait until
it's snowing—the larger the flakes, the better.

   In the middle of a snowfall, take the snow
catcher outside and catch snowflakes on it.
Examine with the magnifying glass.

What happens:

Because the snow catcher is cold, the snowflakes won't melt the way they often do on your jacket. You should have plenty of time to examine them. How many different kinds of snowflakes can you find?

Why:

What shape a snowflake will take depends mostly on the temperature and how much water there is in the clouds (humidity), while how big the snowflake gets depends mostly on humidity. Generally, the more water there is in the air high up from the earth (atmosphere), the bigger the snowflakes grow.

NAME	SYMBOL	SHAPE
HEXAGONAL PLATES		
STELLAR CRYSTALS		
HEXAGONAL COLUMNS		
NEEDLES		
SPATIAL DENDRITES		
CAPPED COLUMNS		
IRREGULAR CRYSTALS		

4 Soil, Air, and Water

Using Soil to Clean Water

You need:
grape Kool-Aid
large container
3 Styrofoam coffee or soup cups
a pencil
1 cup each of soil, pebbles, and sand
tape
4 glasses

What to do:
Make the Kool-Aid (don't add sugar) in the large container and set aside. Poke a hole in the bottom of each cup with a pencil. Fill one cup with the soil, one with the sand, and one with the pebbles. Mark the cups with tape labels reading SOIL, SAND, and PEBBLES. Mark three glasses with the same tape labels, and mark the fourth glass KOOL-AID. Run some fresh water through the filled cups to remove materials that may cloud the Kool-Aid.

Now hold a cup over the glass that matches it (SOIL to SOIL, etc.) and pour the Kool-Aid in, letting it drip through the cup into the glass. Stop before the glass is full. Now pour the Kool-Aid into the second cup, over the second glass, and do the same with the third. Fill the fourth glass with Kool-Aid.

Wait several days to let the particles settle to the bottom of the glass. Compare the colors of the filtered water.

What happens:

Which glass has the lightest liquid? Which has the darkest? How fast did the Kool-Aid travel through each cup?

Why:

Chances are the Kool-Aid that went through the soil became the clearest or cleanest. This is actually how water from our houses gets cleaned: It drains into soil and, as it drips down through the layers of soil to lakes and rivers underground, the soil acts as a filter, cleaning the water.

Make a Landfill Bucket

You need:

an assortment of items: include something plastic,
    a piece of Styrofoam, a piece of fabric or paper,
    a piece of fruit or fruit/vegetable peel,
    cereal, etc. (no meat—that would smell)
        a notebook
        a pencil
        a big bucket of slightly moist soil

What to do:

Make a list of what you've collected.
Bury all the items in the bucket, putting
all the things that have been alive on one side.
Keep the soil moist by watering it several times a week. If it's
summer, check in one month and see what's begun to fall apart
(decompose). If it's winter, put the bucket in a warm spot and
check in two months. Compare what has begun to fall apart and
what hasn't. Compare food with paper and plastic.

What happens:

Just like logs and dead animals, food will rot and eventually fall apart. Why? Because insects, worms, snails, slugs, and little critters too small for our eyes to see (they're microscopic) eat them and food falls apart. Then earthworms and other burrowing creatures mix up the soil. Chances are the food has rotted while the plastic hasn't changed at all. Paper might also show some signs of rotting.

Why:

The little creatures in the soil eat the food and, in doing so, help break it down. But they can't eat plastic. Food will completely disappear over the course of months (peels of fruits take longer, but bread and cereal should disappear quickly). Landfills are full of plastic, metal, and other objects that just pile up; some never decompose. Will we eventually just have acres and acres of land filled with garbage?

Garbage and More Garbage

The typical American throws out 4 pounds (2 kilograms) of garbage every day. If we consider how much is thrown out all over the country, including what companies and factories throw out, it adds up to 40 pounds (18 kilograms) of garbage per person every day—millions of tons every year. That's a lot of junk!

That's why recycling paper, glass, cans, and kitchen waste is so important .

5 Leaves, Plants, Seeds, and Spores

Growing Mr. or Ms. Grasshead

You need:

3 paper or plastic cups that you can
    draw on (Styrofoam cups are good)
a pencil
potting soil
cotton balls
grass seed or watercress seeds
2 plastic bags big enough to put the cups
    in, with twists

What to do:

Draw a funny or happy face on each cup.
Make them as detailed as you like but don't
give them hair. With a pencil, poke a hole in
the bottom of two cups and fill them with soil to about 1 inch
(2.5 cm) from the top. Fill the third with cotton to the same level—
1 inch (2.5 cm) from the rim of the cup.

    Make the soil and cotton very moist with water.

    Sprinkle the seeds so they create a full single layer over the soil
and cotton. Be sure to sprinkle seeds close to the edge of the cup
too.

    Cover with ½ inch (1 cm) of soil or cotton and moisten—do not
soak with water.

    Cover one of the cups filled with soil and the cup filled with
cotton with plastic bags and close with a twist. Leave plenty of
empty space in the bag just above the soil.

    Put the three cups near a sunny window and lightly sprinkle
with water every other day.

What happens:

How long does it take before you see a sprout? Which cup is the first to have sprouts? Why? What do you notice on the inside of the plastic bag in several days? How did droplets get there? Why do the seeds grow on cotton? Do you think the plants will live longer and healthier in the soil or cotton? Why?

Why:

Chances are the grass in the plastic bag with the soil grew the fastest because the bag keeps the plants warm and moist. The water you put in the soil and cotton went into the air (evaporated) and then collected on the bag. That gave the plants their own little rain cloud.

The cotton gives the plants a place to grow, but it doesn't have as many nutrients (food) as the soil has. That's why the grass will probably be healthier in the soil.

Our Grassy Diets, by Julia Schneider, age 11

Grass for breakfast, grass for lunch, and grass for dinner, too! Wheat, corn, oats, rice, and sugarcane are grasses. From them we make cereals, bagels, most breads, macaroni, some candies, and vinegar. Many things we use, including glue, laundry starch, and paste are made from rice. Types of grass are also used to heat homes and build houses, rafts, bridges, furniture, and fishing poles; even some plastics are made from grass such as bamboo. Grass grows just about every place all over the world, from snowy mountains and soggy swamps to jungles and even dry deserts.

Make a Spore Print

You need:
a late summer or early fall day
    near some woods
mushrooms or toadstools
a pair of scissors
a box
white or colored paper
glue stick or rubber cement
a bowl
plastic fixative, spray adhesive, or hair spray (optional)

What to do:
Take a walk in the woods and collect several large umbrella-shaped mushrooms. Cut the stems off with scissors and put them in a box to carry. At home, cut the rest of the stems off. You'll be left with the mushroom cap. Examine underneath the cap and notice all the "gills"—the little lines with spaces between them.

If the cap is lightly colored choose a darker-colored paper. If it's dark, use white paper. Spread a thin layer of the glue or rubber cement in the center of the paper. Spread it just a bit larger than the mushroom you're going to use. Place the mushroom cap on the paper, gill side down, with a bowl over it for a few hours or overnight. *Wash your hands after handling mushrooms.*

What happens:

When you remove the bowl and mushroom cap, you'll notice a beautiful pattern made from the mushroom spores. If you want to preserve it, you can spray it with plastic fixative or spray adhesive.

Why:

A typical mushroom might release as many as 30 million spores. An ink cap fungus—common on lawns and animal droppings—has been known to produce 5 billion spores in just two days; that's more than a million a minute!

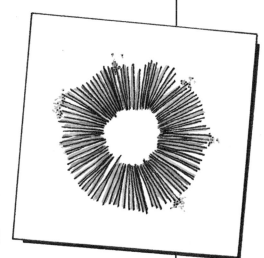

Fungi Feeding

Like plants, mushrooms and other fungi can't move around. Like animals, they can't produce their own food. And like insects, fungi are made out of the same tough material that insects' hard skeletons are made of. Yet fungi are different from all of them. Fungi are nature's cleanup crew, breaking down all kinds of organic materials so nature can use them again. Fungi grow thin white threadlike tubes that ooze out chemicals that help break their food down, just like our saliva. The main part of the fungi is underground. Mushrooms and other growths we see above ground are there for only one reason: to produce and release the thousands or millions of spores that will float in the wind trying to find a place to grow.

Make It a Dandelion and Daisy Day

You need:
plenty of sprouting dandelions
several pencils
paper
a patch of daisies

What to do:
Find three dandelion plants to study. You'll want plants with flower buds still hidden in the center of the plant. Stick a pencil next to each plant and mark the flower's height on the pencil. Take notes three times a day and try to answer these questions: How quickly do the flower stalks grow? How many days does it take for a dandelion bud to blossom? Do you notice the flower closed in the morning, open in the afternoon, and then closed up for the night?

What happens:
Dandelions grow incredibly fast. You should be able to notice a difference day by day.

Why:
Dandelions are one of the most rugged weeds. If they get mowed down, they're back up again in just a day or two. Although some dandelions die in one year, many live for two.

Dandelions are called lion's teeth in French (*dents-de-lion*), because if you look at the leaves sideways, they look like the teeth of a lion.

One dandelion plant produces thousands of seeds that take off when the flower head becomes a fluff ball. The seeds are attached to delicate parachutes that drift in the breeze.

Make a Daisy Garland, Crown, or Necklace

Pick a bunch of daisies, keeping the stems long. Put one flower down on a table sideways (horizontal). Now take another and put it down so it's lying straight (vertical) over the sideways stem. Loop the vertical stem behind the first flower and then over itself. Pull gently to tighten the loop and push the head of the second flower sideways, next to the first flower. Now take a third flower and lay it vertically on top of the other two stems. Repeat the loop. When you have the length you want, make a circle by tucking the loose stems from one end into the loops of the other end.

Spatter Print Note Cards or Bookmarks

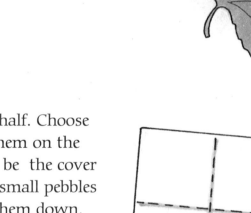

You need:
an old shirt to cover your
    clothes—tempera stains!
heavy paper or cardboard
a pencil
a collection of fresh leaves
pennies or small pebbles
tempera or poster paint,
    thinned with a little water
a saucer
an old toothbrush
a comb or knife

What to do:
For note cards, fold paper in half. Choose
one or more leaves and lay them on the
section of the paper that will be the cover
of your card. Put pennies or small pebbles
on top of the leaves to hold them down.
Try to weigh down the tips of the leaves
so your edges will be sharply defined.

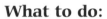

    Pour some paint into a saucer. Dip the
toothbrush in the paint and tap off the
excess. Hold the toothbrush at an angle pointing downward to the
paper, bristles up. With the comb or knife, pull along the bristles
toward you. As the bristles snap back into place, they will splash

paint on the leaves and paper. Be sure to pull the toothbrush toward you so the splatter shoots away from you. Turn your paper to be sure you cover the whole piece. You may want to try adding a second color. Let dry and carefully remove leaf or leaves. Experiment with several colors.

Different Leaf Print Note Cards or Bookmarks

You need:
crayons or colored pencils
a collection of old or new leaves
paper

Fold your paper as before. Take the paper wraps off the crayons you'd like to use. Arrange your choice of leaves on a flat surface with the undersides (bumpy veins) facing up. Unfold your paper and carefully lay it on top of the arranged leaves. The front of your card should be facing up, with the back on the leaves. Rub the sides of the crayons over the whole front of your card.

Pollen's Powder's Got Power!

You need:
a piece of black velvet or corduroy
scissors
a piece of cardboard
tape
any kind of flowers (If it's winter,
    ask a florist for flowers being
    thrown out; if it's summer, find
    flowers you'd like to use. You
    don't need to pick them.)

What to do:
Cut the fabric 1 inch (2.5 cm) larger than the cardboard on all
sides. Wrap the edges of the fabric over the cardboard and tape
them onto the back. Gently rub or press the flower bud against the
board. Don't crush the flower. Compare the amount of pollen you
collect from different flowers.

What happens:
Pollen will easily slip off the flower and show up on your board.
The amount and colors of the pollen should be different from
flower to flower.

**MAGNIFIED
POLLEN GRAINS**

Why:

Flowers are chock full of pollen because that's how plants reproduce. Just as two animals must come together to create a baby, most flowers need other flowers to grow seeds.

But flowers can't move, so they've developed a different way to make "baby" plants. Most have both female parts (pistils) and male parts (stamens) which produce pollen—sticky powderlike grains.

The female part of a flower needs a male's pollen from another flower to produce a seed. This occurs when the pollen is blown to it by the wind, or brought to it by insects and birds that visit to enjoy some of its sweet nectar. While dining, the insects' and birds' legs and bodies pick up some sticky pollen, and when they fly off to another flower, some of the pollen sticks to the new flower and fertilizes it. Now the flower can make seeds for new plants.

Trees Breathe Out Enough Water to Fill a Swimming Pool Each Year

You need:
2 twigs with 4 to 7 leaves on each
a ruler
4 glasses or plastic cups
permanent black marker or tape
food coloring
vegetable oil

What to do:
With the ruler, mark the inches (or centimeters) up the side of each cup or glass using a permanent black marker or pieces of tape. Fill each glass three-quarters full of water. Add several drops of food coloring to one glass. Add a layer of oil to prevent evaporation. Put a twig in the glass. In glass two, with clear water, add a layer of oil and the other twig. In glass three, with clear water, add a layer of oil. In glass four, don't add anything to the water. A day later, compare the water levels. Check again in several days.

What happens:
The water can't evaporate because of the oil. Yet water from the glasses with the twigs slowly disappears. Where do you think it goes? Do the leaves in the colored water look any different than when you started the experiment? Compare the clear water glass and the colored water glass.

Why:

The roots of trees suck up water from the ground. The water flows up through little tubes in the tree trunk. Once it reaches the leaves, the leaves can make food, which travels back in different tubes in the trunk so the tree can grow new wood and bark. Extra water passes out of the leaves, which, in turn, draws more water up from the ground.

Trees Are Part of Water's Cycle

Plants need plenty of water too, but without mouths how do they get it? They pull it up from their roots and then breathe out what they don't need. A tree looks quiet and still, but on a summer day water is traveling up through trunks as fast as 3 feet (1 meter) a minute. A full-grown apple tree pulls up about 4 gallons (15 liters) of water every hour from the ground—that's 96 gallons (363 liters) a day. A large oak tree needs and gives off about 110 gallons (416 liters) a day; that's 40,000 gallons (151,400 liters) of water a year—enough to fill a large swimming pool!

The trunk or wood of a tree is about one-half water. Human beings are almost two-thirds water, and elephants are almost three-quarters water! Many vegetables are almost all water.

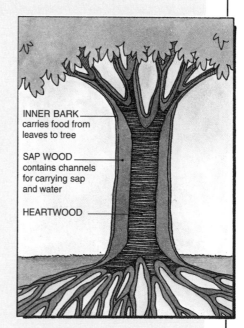

INNER BARK carries food from leaves to tree

SAP WOOD contains channels for carrying sap and water

HEARTWOOD

Other Books You Might Like

Durrell, Gerald. *A Practical Guide for the Amateur Naturalist*. Knopf, 1988.

Exploring Nature with Your Child. Time-Life, 1988.

Lingelback, Jenepher. *Hands On Nature*. Vermont Institute of Natural Science,1986.

Pringle, Laurence. *Discovering the Outdoors*. Natural History Press, 1969.

————. *Discovering Nature Outdoors*. Natural History Press, 1969.

————. *Discovering Nature Indoors: A Nature and Science Guide to Investigations with Small Animals*. Doubleday, 1970.

Sisson, Edith A. *Nature with Children of All Ages*. Prentice-Hall, Inc.

Walker, Dr. Richard. *Nature Project on File*. Facts on File, 1992.

Index

About the Author and Illustrator

Susan S. Lang is a senior science writer at Cornell University in Ithaca, New York. She is a former children's librarian and the author of ten other books and more than 125 articles for national magazines. This is her third children's book.

Cayuga Nature Center is a private, not-for-profit residential environmental educational center in Ithaca, New York. Its programs include education for area schools, nature day camps, seasonal festivals, teacher-training workshops, and developing farms. The center's rustic lodge is set on 135 acres of woods, fields, streams, and ravines.

Sharon Lane Holm won awards for her work in advertising design before shifting her concentration to children's books. Her illustrations have since added zest to books for both the trade and educational markets. She lives in New Fairfield, Connecticut.

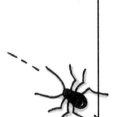